Mat 13:34

All these things spake Jesus unto the multitude in parables; and without a parable spake he not unto them:

Mat 13:35

That it might be fulfilled which was spoken by the prophet, saying, I will open my mouth in parables; I will utter things which have been kept secret from the foundation of the world.

Parables of Jesus Christ

Retold

This story is a work of fiction, and does not pretend, in any way, to be anything else. The people, places, and events in this story were inspired by people, places, and events from the Holy Bible.

Deborah Anne Barrd

ISBN-13: 978-0692426791
(*Home of the Barrd*)

ISBN-10: 0692426795

Barrd of Angels

©2015
Home of the Barrd

All rights reserved. No part of this book may be used or reproduced in any manner whatsoever without written permission of the publisher except in the case of brief quotations embodied in critical articles and reviews.

For more information, contact the Barrd

barrd.of.angels@gmail.com

This Book
is
Lovingly Dedicated
to
True Seekers
of
Wisdom
Everywhere

Parable of the Prodigal Son

2

Part I
The Son

The pleasures of the flesh are calling
His young heart stops to listen
A siren song his ears enthralling
A dream of lips that glisten
A little wine to ease his heart
A little song to make him merry
Arms that open, thighs that part
His misgivings he will bury
His passion and his money spent
He awakens all alone

No swaying breasts, no flashing hips
His companions all are gone
"Why?" he cries to cold deaf ears
He's homeless, cold and hungry
"No one cares, no one hears
The city is heartless and lonely!"
He thinks of the family he left behind
He thinks of the hearts he left broken
What kind of welcome could he find
When no goodbyes were spoken?
And now, with nowhere else to go
His thoughts toward home keep turning
To face a future he doesn't know
At the prodigal's returning.

Part II
The Father

He sits at the window, a broken man
Forgotten, gray and old
Remembering the touch of a tiny hand
As memory grows cold
Listening in silent dread
As if all hope were gone
For the old familiar tread
The old familiar song
Oh, where, oh where is the little boy
Where my darling one?

What happened to the boundless joy
My precious, long lost son?
Has he forgotten home and family
Now that he is grown?
The father's love, the mother's kiss
Has he left us all alone?
Noisy rooms gone quiet now
No need to shout, "Behave!"
No merry laughter, no prayers to hear
All is quiet as the grave.
Is he lost? Or is he dead?
Oh, how his heart is yearning!
His deepest, his most earnest prayer
For the prodigal's returning.

Part III
The Homecoming

There, on the deserted road
A figure walks alone
Bent as if by a heavy load
His weary steps toward home
And, there, in the window, a head comes up
And unbelieving tears
Come coursing down the withered cheek
Forgotten, the bitter years
"Father!" comes the timid voice
"My son!" the joyous cry

"My lost child, you're home at last!
A happy man am I!"
"My Father, I am sorry
for all the wrong I've done"
"My child, all is forgiven,
Welcome home, my son!"
The hillside echoes their joyous cries
As angels dance about the pair
They look into each others eyes
And see the love reflected there
Forgotten, all the lonely years
Forgotten, temptation's burning
Forgotten, the sorrow; forgotten, the tears
At the prodigal's returning.

Part IV
The Jealous Brother

"Now, let us kill the fatted calf!
And let the guests arrive!
For he who was lost is now found
He who was dead, alive!"
Now, as the feast was carried out
With generous libation
With merry laughter, joyous shouts
And wondrous celebration
Another son, in agony
Was watching, all alone

"My father has forgotten me
Me, his loyal son."
"My son, my son", his father said
"Come, now, let's rejoice!
For he's alive, who once was dead!
Now, hearken to my voice!"
"For him you kill the fatted calf
For me, what have you done?"
"Why, everything I have is yours
My faithful, loving son."
He wouldn't see, he wouldn't hear
His heart, with jealous churning
Would not accept his father's joy
At the prodigal's returning.

Part V
The Moral

And now, in sorrow, our Father waits
And watches from above
As we follow the wicked siren's song
His heart breaks with His love
We chase our golden idols
We ignore His broken plea
We follow after every lust
Our hearts cannot be free
With ears gone deaf, and eyes gone blind
Allured by worldly pleasure

We close our hearts, we close our mind
Upon our greatest Treasure
The feast is ready, He paid the price
He extends a loving hand
Will we accept His sacrifice?
Oh, will we understand?
And will we share His happiness
As the lost ones stumble home?
Or seethe with inward bitterness
And wander off, alone?
He stands before the open gates
His heart, with patient yearning
And so our Father sadly waits
For the prodigal's returning.

Saga of a Tiny Seed

Saga of a Tiny Seed

The Sower came, scattering His Seed
And a tiny Seed fell from His Hand
Fell in a rather desperate place
A hard, and a rocky land

The Seed sent its roots down and down
Pushing through much heavy toil
Pushing through the rocks and stones
Till, finally, it found fertile soil

A tender Plant began to grow
Tiny shoots began to appear
But soon it was smothered with many
Weeds
Called Lust and Greed, named Doubt and
Fear

They struggled for space on that rocky ground
For water and sunshine and air
And soon the Plant began to grow tall
And to crowd out the Weeds of Despair

But as soon as Buds began to show
And the Plant began to thrive
A terrible drought turned the green to
brown
Soon the Plant was barely alive

Again the roots reached down and down
    Till they came to a Living Fountain
The plant became nourished by the Water
              of Life
And grew strong upon God's Mountain

    Now there is a Mighty Tree
    Where once was a desolate place
Weary travelers are welcomed to rest in it's
             shade
And to share there in God's Loving Grace

The Poor Widow

20

The Poor Widow

Jesus and His followers went to the
temple for to pray
For the Master had a lesson He would
teach them on that day
They stood and watched as many mighty
leaders in that town
Came to the place of sacrifice, and laid
their money down

Jesus smiled at His disciples, as they all
gasped at what they saw
He said "Gentlemen, please close your
mouths. Don't stare at them in awe.
For these are men who take much pride in
all the things they've got.
You think that they are noble men, but I
tell you, they are not.
But look there, in that corner. There's a
lady you don't know.
Watch and I will tell you of the great
faith she will show."
They stood and watched with bated breath
as she approached the bin
They turned puzzled faces to the Lord as
she dropped two pennies in.

He said "Those proud and wealthy men
gave what they thought they could afford
They gave a tiny pittance from their vast
and mighty hoard.
But that little widow standing there, that
you look at with such scorn
She in faded, ragged dress, looking lonely
and forlorn
I say to you, My faithful friends, she is
beloved of God
And He has sent His angels to guard
every path she'll trod
Her days will be filled with gladness,
Satan will not make her sad
For I say to you, that in her want, she
has given all she had."

The Pharisee and The Publican

 26

The Pharisee and The Publican

Two men went to the synagogue
To offer up their prayers to God
Men as different as could be
A publican and a Pharisee
And as they went along their way
The Lord did listen to them pray

The Pharisee looked up with pride
"Thank You, Lord" he loudly cried
"For I am a man among the best
Separated from the rest
I am better than most other men
Even than this publican"

The publican fell to his knees
"Lord, have mercy on me, please!
For my sin I bear the blame
Oh, Lord, I cannot hide my shame!
Forgive a sinner such as I!
Oh, Lord, I beg You, hear my cry"

Which prayer, then, did the Good Lord hear
Which heart the Holy One hold dear?
Who went back down to his place
Justified before God's face
"Humble yourself", the Savior said
For the Lord will raise the humble head

 30

Invitation to a Feast

32

Invitation to a Feast

A great lord once made a feast
And invited from the west and east
All his friends, both great and small
To celebrate with one and all
And as he sent his servant out
To gather them from round about
They began to fret and moan
Wishing to be left alone

"I have bought a piece of ground
I go to see if it is sound"
"Of oxen I have bought five pair
I must see the dealing fair"
"I have married a new wife
She is the marvel of my life"
The servant suffered this abuse
Listening to each excuse
He went back with his report
And his lord then did retort
"They would make my feast a waste
My supper shall they never taste

Go then, out into the byways
And gather in from off the highways
The poor, the lame, the halt, the blind
Call in all that you shall find"
To you extends this invitation
To the Good Lord's celebration
So leave your worldly cares behind
For in the Lord's House you will find
Peace and joy, beyond measure
Far above all this world's treasure
For your soul, you will find rest
So come, and be His royal guest

 36

The Parable of the Good Samaritan

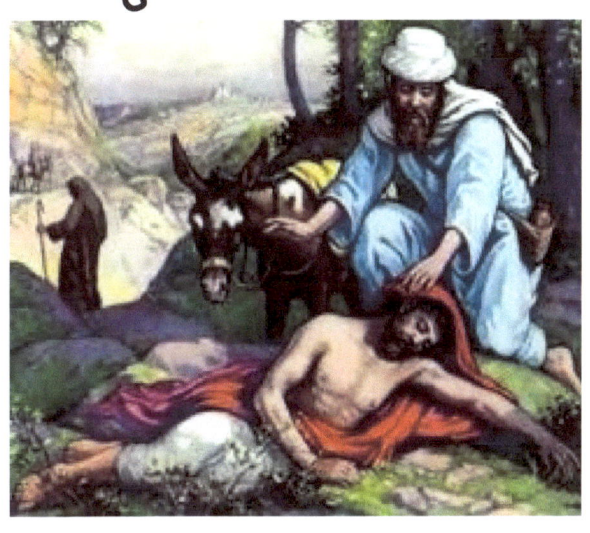

The Parable of the Good Samaritan

Part I

There, along the Jericho road
He traveled all alone
Without friend or companion
Completely on his own
Oblivious, he traveled toward
A vicious, evil fate
For up ahead, with greedy plan
Wicked men did wait
Steep hills surrounded every side
Along the winding way
And as he passed beneath their lair
They leaped upon their prey
They beat him, and they robbed him
From many wounds he bled
His cries for help unanswered
They left him then for dead

Part II

Another traveler happened by
A man of priestly bearing
Who heard the piteous, helpless cry
While to the city faring
"I cannot help this man," he though
"Not for God's Holy Name
Blood upon my priestly robes
Why it would be a shame
So they left him lying there
Defenseless, unprotected
Until a Levite came that way
A revered man and respected
"I cannot stop and offer aid
I haven't got the time!
Besides, it just might compromise
The office that is mine!"

Part III

And so they left him all alone
With no hope of survival
Until a Samaritan came along
A despised and hated rival
He saw the victim lying there
And felt, within his breast
A glimmer of God's loving care
And so he gave his best
He soothed the man; he bound his wounds
With oil and with wine
He said, "Sir, ride upon my beast
All that I have is thine"
He took him to him to a local inn
And tended him with care
He saw to each and every need
Before he left him there

Part IV

Who was a neighbor to this man?
And which one was a friend?
Now go and do thou likewise
Unto thy journey's end
Listen to the Lord's command
Heed His loving call
He has blessed His children
With love for one and all
Do not walk life's highway
Filled with earthly greed
But be prepared to lend a hand
When you see someone in need
If you would be with Jesus
The heavenly stair ascend
Treat each man as your brother
And each man as your friend

The Lost Sheep

The Lost Sheep

One little lamb of the Master's flock
He loved his Shepherd so
A mischievous lamb, a curious lamb
He was always on the go
Following after each new thing
That he found along the way
And often it happened the lamb would get lost
And wander far astray

And though the Shepherd had much to do
What with a hundred sheep
Each time His little lamb got lost
The Good Shepherd would go and seek
There, out in the wilderness
He'd leave the ninety and nine
To search for His one precious little lamb
Who had been left behind
Patiently and lovingly
He'd search among the rocks
Until He found His little lost lamb
And returned him to the flock

He'd carry him upon His shoulders
His joy a delight to behold
For His little lamb was home again
Safe within His fold
Was it me the Lord was thinking of
As He told this little tale
A story of a Heavenly Kingdom to come
Of His Love which will never fail

*Praise
the Lord,
my soul;*
all my inmost being,
praise His holy Name.
Praise the Lord,
my soul,
and forget not all
His benefits –
who forgives all your sins
and heals all your diseases,
who redeems your life
from the pit
and crowns you with love
and compassion,
who satisfies your desires
with good things
so that your youth is
renewed like the eagle's.

Psalm 103.1-5